THREE MASS PROPER CYCLES
FROM JENA 35

RECENT RESEARCHES IN THE MUSIC OF THE RENAISSANCE

James Haar and Howard Mayer Brown, general editors

A-R Editions, Inc., publishes six quarterly series—

Recent Researches in the Music of the Middle Ages and Early Renaissance,
Margaret Bent, general editor;

Recent Researches in the Music of the Renaissance,
James Haar and Howard Mayer Brown, general editors;

Recent Researches in the Music of the Baroque Era,
Robert L. Marshall, general editor;

Recent Researches in the Music of the Classical Era,
Eugene K. Wolf, general editor;

Recent Researches in the Music of the Nineteenth and Early Twentieth Centuries,
Rufus Hallmark, general editor;

Recent Researches in American Music,
H. Wiley Hitchcock, general editor—

which make public music that is being brought to light
in the course of current musicological research.

Each volume in the *Recent Researches* is devoted
to works by a single composer or to a single genre of composition,
chosen because of its potential interest to scholars and performers,
and prepared for publication according to the standards that govern
the making of all reliable historical editions.

Correspondence should be addressed:

A-R EDITIONS, INC.
315 West Gorham Street
Madison, Wisconsin 53703

RECENT RESEARCHES IN THE MUSIC OF THE RENAISSANCE • VOLUME LIII

THREE
MASS PROPER CYCLES

from Jena 35

Edited by Robert E. Gerken

A-R EDITIONS, INC. • MADISON

Copyright © 1982, A-R Editions, Inc.
ISSN 0486-123X
ISBN 0-89579-165-X

Library of Congress Cataloging in Publication Data:
Main entry under title:
Three Mass Proper cycles from Jena 35.

   (Recent researches in the music of the
Renaissance , ISSN 0486-123X ; v. 53)
   For chorus (SATB)
   Latin words.
   The works are anonymous.
   Edited from choirbook 35 in the Jena University
Library.
   Contents: Mass for Easter Sunday—Mass for Whit
Monday—Mass for Feasts of the Blessed Virgin
Mary.
   1. Propers (Music)   I. Gerken, Robert E.
II. Friedrich-Schiller-Universität Jena. Bibliothek.
Manuscript. 35.   III. Series.
M2.R2384   vol. 53   [M2014.5]   783.2′3   82-13762
ISBN 0-89579-165-X

Contents

Mass for Feasts of the Blessed Virgin Mary

Preface

The Jena Choirbooks

Until fairly recently, the Mass Proper cycles of Trent Codex 88 and those found in Isaac's *Choralis Constantinus* were thought to be the only extensive Proper cycles from the fifteenth and early sixteenth centuries. However, the publication of *Die geistlichen Musikhandschriften der Universitäts-Bibliothek Jena* (1935) by Karl Erich Roediger brought to light yet a third group of Mass Proper cycles, namely, those contained in the Jena choirbooks. These manuscript choirbooks are preserved in the Jena University Library, where they form part of a collection of sixteenth-century music consisting of eighteen choirbooks and sixty-three printed partbooks. The choirbooks bear the numbers 2-5, 7-9, 12, 20-22, and 30-36 in this collection. Although the choirbooks are maintained in the Jena University Library, the music they contain has no connection with the musical history of Jena and originally belonged to Frederick the Wise, Elector of Saxony at Wittenberg (1486-1525). In the discussion that follows, the choirbooks will be referred to by the numbers assigned to them within the larger Jena collection.

Three of the thirteen complete Mass Proper cycles contained in Jena 35 have been selected for inclusion in the present edition. Two of these, the *Mass for Easter Sunday* and the *Mass for Feasts of the Blessed Virgin Mary*, are the most impressive Masses of the entire manuscript. They are the only cycles that incorporate parts of the Mass Ordinary. In addition, their Kyries, Glorias, and Sequences are clear-cut examples of *alternatim* movements, since the polyphonic settings provided are only for alternate verses of these movements. The third cycle, the *Mass for Whit Monday*, was selected because it is typical of the cycles in Jena 35, both in its musical style and in the parts selected for polyphonic treatment.[1]

Ten of the eighteen Jena choirbooks, nos. 2-5, 7-9, 12, 20, and 22, are sumptuous vellum manuscripts, surpassed in their dimensions only by the concordances in the Sistine Chapel.[2] These ten all derive from the Saxon Court, but were probably finished in the Netherlands in the second decade of the sixteenth century. They are made up largely of settings of the Mass Ordinary, single Mass movements, and Requiem Masses. Choirbook 20 is exceptional in that it contains settings of the Magnificat. Most of the compositions in the vellum manuscripts are ascribed; they are by Josquin Desprez, Pierre de La Rue, and their contemporaries. These ten choirbooks are especially valuable for study of the work of Pierre de La Rue.

Choirbook 4, with a format of 78 x 54.5 cm., must be among the largest choirbooks in the world.[3] Along with Choirbook 9, it was originally intended for Henry VIII of England. These two choirbooks were acquired by Maximilian and, together with Choirbook 7, were given to Frederick the Wise as a gift in 1518. The Maximilian choirbooks (nos. 4, 7, and 9) are lavishly decorated with miniatures in the style of such masters as Hans Memling, Rogier van der Weyden, and Hugo van der Goes.[4]

The eight remaining Jena choirbooks, nos. 21, 30-36, are paper manuscripts. One additional paper manuscript, Stadtkirche Weimar A, should be added to this last group,[5] since it was originally part of the collection belonging to Frederick. From a study of the script and contents of these paper manuscripts, Roediger concludes that, with the exception of Choirbook 21, they were written for the Saxon Court Chapel of Frederick the Wise in the first two decades of the sixteenth century.[6] They provide a valuable insight into the liturgical music of the Saxon Court Chapel on the eve of the Reformation. Choirbooks 21, 31, 32, and 36 contain compositions setting the Ordinary of the Mass, and Choirbook 34 contains settings of the Proper for Vespers.

On the basis of style and script, the paper manuscripts fall into three groups, of which the first is the largest. Group one contains Choirbooks 30-33 and Weimar A, and in this group, compositions ascribed to Adam Rener and Heinrich Isaac are found. Group two includes Choirbooks 34 and 35. The final group is made up of Choirbook 36 alone; it includes Mass Ordinary compositions by Isaac and Rener.

Choirbooks 34 and 35 have in common the non-mensural (chant) notation of their tenors. Choirbook 34 contains settings of psalms, antiphons, hymns, and responsories for Vespers of the chief feasts in the Wittenberg calendar. These works are in the style of harmonized psalm settings that "bring the essence of Gregorian psalmody to an even stronger expression in the polyphony."[7] Choirbook 35 contains ninety-two Proper compositions, most of which are included in thirteen Mass Proper cycles arranged in the order of the church year beginning with Easter. The cycles are Masses from the Proper of the Time or Masses of the Blessed Virgin Mary.

Adam Rener and the Jena 35 Mass Proper Cycles

Adam Rener has recently emerged as an important composer of polyphonic Mass Proper cycles, a genre dominated by Heinrich Isaac.[8] Most of the ascribed compositions in Jena 30 and 36 are by Rener or Isaac. Moreover, four polyphonic Mass Proper cycles by Rener are included in Rhau's publication of 1545, *Officiorum . . . de nativitate, circumcisione, epiphania Domini et purificatione*.[9] Three of these four cycles are different settings of the same text, the *Mass for the Nativity of Our Lord*. The third of these Nativity cycles is found as an anonymous work in Jena 35, but on the basis of the attribution in the Rhau publication, it is ascribed to Adam Rener. All other cycles in both Jena 30 and 35, which contain only Mass Proper cycles, are anonymous; however, they closely resemble the style of the works in this genre attributed to Adam Rener.

In determining ascription to Rener, it is significant to note that Rener used a more progressive approach to the *cantus firmus* in his Magnificat compositions and Mass Ordinary settings than he did in his settings of the Proper of the Mass.[10] Rener's manipulation of the borrowed plainsong melody in his polyphonic Mass Proper cycles corresponds very closely to the method employed in the anonymous cycles of Jena 30.[11] In fact, not only in *cantus firmus* treatment, but also in general musical style and in the structural relations between the polyphonic setting and its plainsong model, the cycles of Jena 30 and 35 and the one attributed to Rener in the Rhau publication show a similar style.

If we may trust Rhau's ascription to Rener of the *Mass for the Nativity of Our Lord*—and there seems to be no reason to doubt it, considering Rener's contemporary reputation and his position as *Kapellmeister* to Frederick the Wise between 1507 and 1517—then it is virtually certain that other settings of the Mass Proper in Jena 30 and 35 are also by Rener. Not only individual Proper settings, but even entire cy-

cles in addition to the Nativity cycle are probably by Rener. In the present edition, the *Mass for Whit Monday* shows a consistently high level of musical quality throughout and a mastery of the strict style of setting a *cantus firmus* worthy of Adam Rener. The Introits in the *Mass for Easter Sunday* and in the *Mass for Feasts of the Blessed Virgin Mary* not only equal that for the *Mass of the Nativity of Our Lord*, but even surpass it in quality. In the section below, "Characteristics and Style of the Jena 35 Mass Proper Cycles," specific passages from the three Masses of this edition are cited in demonstration of the high quality of composition typical of Rener.

Adam Rener was born ca. 1485 in Liège, and in 1498 he was a choirboy in the court chapel of Maximilian I.[12] In 1500, after his voice changed, he was allowed to go to Burgundy to continue his education. After three years there, he returned to the Imperial Chapel as a composer, but left in 1507 to go to Torgau to succeed Adam von Fulda as *Kapellmeister* in the Chapel of the Saxon Elector Frederick the Wise. He is mentioned several times in the roster of the Electoral Chapel and in various other documents that date from just after 1507.[13] Rener was court composer to Frederick until 1517; he died three years later in Altenburg.

A personal acquaintance between Rener and Isaac is assumed, since Isaac was Maximilian's court composer from 1496 until 1515, and, therefore, had close connections with Maximilian's chapel, as well. Next to Isaac, Rener was probably the most significant Franco-Netherlandish composer in Germany in the early sixteenth century.[14] It was with Rener's appointment to the Court Chapel of Frederick that liturgical music in nearby Wittenberg rose above the provinciality to which it had been relegated, even under Adam von Fulda.

Liturgical Music in Wittenberg

Wittenberg is best remembered as the cradle of the Reformation and for its close connection with Martin Luther. In 1486 Frederick the Wise succeeded his father as the Elector of Saxony. In 1502 he founded the University of Wittenberg, and later he invited Luther and Melanchthon to teach there. After Luther had been excommunicated and made an outlaw by the imperial ban of 1521, he was sheltered by Frederick at the Wartburg castle. Frederick was sympathetic to Luther's ideas, but he was opposed to the iconoclastic tendencies of some of Luther's followers, such as Karlstadt (Andreas Bodenstein). In view of the unsettled religious conditions in Wittenberg at this time, it should be noted that the music of Jena 35 (copied ca. 1500-1520) is definitely Roman Catholic liturgical music. Radical liturgical changes in Wittenberg did not commence until 1521, while Luther was in hiding and Karlstadt was archdeacon of the castle Church of All Saints.

In pre-Reformation Wittenberg (before 1520), as was typical at this time, plainsong was the foundation of the Roman Catholic liturgical music. The Offices and the ferial services were sung in choral unison. Fauxbourdon was improvised on special occasions falling on ferial days, and polyphony was provided for Sundays and feast days.[15] In addition to the large choir, a small choir was established by Frederick in 1506 for the special veneration of the Virgin. (In this emphasis, Frederick was in line with the prevailing sympathies of the age.) In addition to the Mass of the Day, a Marian Mass was celebrated daily according to the following plan:

Sunday: Immaculate Conception
Monday: Nativity of the Virgin
Tuesday: Presentation of the Virgin in the Temple
Wednesday: Annunciation
Thursday: Visitation
Friday: Seven Sorrows of Mary or Purification of the Virgin
Saturday: In Memory of the Virgin or Death of the Virgin

The veneration of the Virgin in the Offices and during Lent was governed by detailed instructions,[16] and the veneration of the Mother of the Virgin, St. Anne, also played an important role in the liturgy of All Saints Church, as elsewhere during the early sixteenth century.

Toward the end of 1524, however, because of Luther's sermons and petitions to the princes, the old service was discontinued at the castle Church. In 1525, High Mass was held in German, and the small choir was disbanded. The services for the Saints were abolished, and the veneration of the Virgin was discontinued.

Characteristics and Style of the Jena 35 Mass Proper Cycles

Jena 35 consists mainly of complete polyphonic Mass Proper cycles from the Proper of the Time and for Marian feasts, arranged in the order of the church year, beginning with Easter Sunday. In addition to these complete cycles, there are several partial cycles and independent movements. In the Jena choirbooks, a complete Mass Proper cycle includes polyphonic settings of plainsong for the Introit, Alleluia, Sequence, and Communion. Two of the complete cycles are exceptional in that they incorporate parts from the Mass Ordinary. These two cycles are the *Mass for Easter Sunday* and the *Mass for Feasts of the Blessed Virgin Mary*, both of which include settings of the Kyrie and Gloria, along with the items of the Proper. In the *Mass for Feasts of the Blessed Virgin Mary*, individual phrases of the Gloria trope "Spiritus et alme" are further incorporated into the traditional liturgical text of the Gloria. As a rule, in the Jena choirbooks (as in Isaac's *Choralis Constantinus*) the Gradual and Offertory are not included in the polyphonic cycles. The only exceptions are the *Mass for Easter Sunday*, in which the Gradual respond is set, and the *Mass for the Feast of the Annunciation*, in which the Gradual verse is set polyphonically.

The outstanding characteristic of the music of Jena 35 is the exclusive use of strict *cantus firmus* technique. In this style, the borrowed melody is presented in one voice, in notes of equal value, and without any rests or any interpolated notes whatsoever. The result of such a procedure is that the plainsong melody is forced into a strait-jacket in which rhythmical life and phrase structure are entirely absent in the voice bearing the *cantus firmus*. In Jena 35, the *cantus firmus* is invariably carried by the tenor, where the plainsong is transformed into an abstract structural foundation with very little melodic value as an independent voice part.

This strict *cantus firmus* technique is an archaic tradition that can be traced back to the discantus sections of the organa and the early Latin motets (with tenors in rhythmic mode 5) of the Notre Dame School. The compositions in English discant style in the Old Hall manuscript afford many examples of settings of this type from the fourteenth and early fifteenth centuries. Apparently settings in this style were not as common in the fifteenth century as those using the discant paraphrase technique; however, examples are abundant in the church music of German composers like Adam von Fulda and Heinrich Finck. In the sixteenth century, a similar approach was adopted and developed by composers of the polyphonic German hymn. Although Isaac made no use of this type of setting, it persisted throughout the sixteenth century.[17]

In Jena 35, the Introit of each Proper cycle is set in two sections corresponding to the plainsong divisions of antiphon and verse. Each section begins with its own intonation. After the verse, the Gloria Patri is sung in plainsong and followed by a restatement of the polyphonic antiphon. The Alleluia is also set in two sections: the Alleluia respond always comes to a full close, after which the much longer verse is set. The typical Sequence is a multi-sectional form wherein the polyphonic sections alternate with plainsong in performance. Usually, the even-numbered verses were set polyphonically. Of all the Proper settings, only the Communion has one continuous section following its intonation. Among the polyphonic Mass Proper forms of Jena 35, the Alleluia alone makes fairly consistent use of thematic unification between its formal divisions. Significantly, this unification is nearly always present already in the plainsong melody, usually in the form of repetition of the *jubilus* at the end of the verse. (See the Alleluia verse in the *Mass for Whit Monday*, where there is a literal repeat of a section of the respond: mm. 84-105 = mm. 11-32.)

Imitation is of very little importance in Jena 35, and when it does occur, it appears almost as an afterthought; imitation never serves any structural purpose in these works. The texture of most movements wavers between strict homophony and non-imitative polyphony. The simplest settings seem to be no more than harmonizations of the *cantus firmus*, while the more complex settings achieve a greater melodic independence in the individual voices, in spite of the rigid adherence to the strict *cantus firmus* technique. The rhythmic activity is fairly evenly distributed among the discant, alto, and bass; but the almost complete absence of imitation and the infrequent use of rests results in a continuous stream of partly embellished homophony that seems to indicate a *horror vacui* on the part of Adam Rener and the other composers of Jena 35.

In most of the movements, the voices move basically in half-notes, those for the discant, alto, and bass having been added to the preexistent tenor *cantus firmus*. The basic half-note motion of the additional voices is embellished in various ways: by skips to notes a quarter-note long, by quarter- and eighth-note passing tones, by occasional chord changes on quarter-note beats, by cross rhythms, and by suspensions. Although a certain amount of variety is provided by these devices, they do not have any structural significance, and the texture, with few exceptions, remains that of continuous, unrelieved homophony.

In the Glorias in the *Mass for Easter Sunday* and in the *Mass for Feasts of the Blessed Virgin Mary*, the words "Jesu Christe" and "suscipe deprecationem nostrum" are given special treatment. In all but one instance of these text settings, the note values of the tenor have been editorially augmented in order for the voices to coincide. The single exception is found in the *Mass for Easter Sunday*, in which the discant, alto, and bass change mensuration from *tempus im-*

perfectum diminutum (₵) to *tempus imperfectum* (c) at the words "suscipe deprecationem nostrum."

In the strict *cantus firmus* style of these settings, there seems to be little doubt that the mode of the tenor is the mode of the polyphonic setting. Because of the different ranges of the voices, no valid distinction between authentic and plagal can be made in these polyphonic modal settings.

In the polyphony of the early sixteenth century, the system of medieval modes was already in the process of transition. This process of modal change can be seen very clearly in the plainsong settings found in Jena 35. Briefly stated, we find the following: (1) the Lydian mode is invariably altered by the addition of one flat to the signature and becomes transposed Ionian; (2) Aeolian and Ionian modes are found, usually in their transposed forms, even though they were not yet recognized by early sixteenth-century theorists; (3) any mode may be transposed, most frequently by shifting the original pitch level of the *cantus firmus* up a fourth and adding one flat to the signature. (Modes are said to be transposed when the pitch level of the plainsong *cantus firmus* in the polyphonic setting differs from its pitch level in modern chant books. The usual reason for such transposition was to allow a wider-ranging bass part below the tenor *cantus firmus*.) Approximately thirty percent of the Proper settings in Jena 35 are in transposed modes, especially transposed Dorian and transposed Ionian. Those polyphonic modal settings that have G as a *finalis* (i.e., Mixolydian and transposed Dorian) account for about sixty percent of all the settings in this source.

In this period it was common for polyphonic Mass cycles to include works by several composers. Thus, if an entire Proper cycle is to be attributed to a single composer, stylistic consistency among movements will provide strong evidence. The treatment of cadences is one feature of style where such consistency may be sought. The following examples of the treatment of the final cadences in various parts of the Proper in the *Mass for Easter Sunday* lend credence to the notion of a single composer for this entire cycle.

The antiphon of the Introit *Resurrexi* is classified in mode 4 in the *Liber Usualis*. The *cantus firmus* has been shifted up a fourth and a flat has been added to the signature in this setting. The final cadence may be described as a cadence on A with the D a fifth lower in the bass. There is no third in the final chord, nor is the suspension formula used at this point. The mode of the plainsong melody for the Alleluia respond as given in the *Liber Usualis* (mode 7) is retained in this setting. The final cadence is on G, and the bass doubles the tenor at the octave. There is no third in the final chord, nor is the suspension dissonance used. The mode of the Sequence plainsong melody as given in Anselm Schubiger *Die Sängerschule St. Gallens vom 8. bis 12. Jahrhundert*[18] is Mixolydian; some of the verses use the range of the authentic mode and others the plagal range. Thus, the Sequence is in *modus mixtus*, the combination of an authentic mode and its own plagal. In seven of the ten sections (verses), the *cantus firmus* cadences on G, and in three, on D. Verse twelve closes with a quite unusual cadence in which the note B-natural is doubled at the octave in the upper voices of the final chord, and the application of *musica ficta* in order to provide a leading tone would be out of the question (see Example 1):

The final cadence of verse ten of the Sequence furnishes us with one of the rare examples of thematic unification among movements in Jena 35. A kind of "motto cadence" relates to the final cadences of the Introit antiphon and the Alleluia respond in the same Mass (see Example 2):

Such thematic interrelations also suggest a single composer of these movements.

Finally, the Communion *Pascha nostrum* retains its tenor *cantus firmus* melody at the same pitch level as that given in the *Liber Usualis* (mode 6), but is in fact in the transposed Ionian mode because of the addition of one flat to the signature of all voice parts. The most striking feature of this setting is the constant use of the suspension dissonance throughout: it occurs seventeen times on F resolving to E, most often in the discant against G in another voice (usually the tenor). The final cadence is on F with no third in the final chord. The bass doubles the tenor at the octave, and the suspension dissonance is not used.

Numerous additional passages in the three Masses presented in this edition could be cited to demonstrate high quality of composition and its relation to works attributed to Adam Rener. For example, notice the fine effect of the "drive to the cadence" at the close of the antiphon in the *Mass for Easter Sunday* (p. 4, mm. 54-59). The final cadence of the Introit verse in the *Mass for Whit Monday* (p. 36, mm. 50-53) affords an example of cadential extension occasionally found in Jena 35.

The Introit *Salve sancta Parens* in the *Mass for Feasts of the Blessed Virgin Mary* has its chief melodic interest in the discant, where the emphasis on G, B-flat, and D suggests a kind of "triadic melody" typical of polyphonic settings in mode 2. This same Introit displays a number of parallel sixths and parallel tenths as well as a finely spun melodic line in the discant to the words "puerpera Regem" (p. 49, mm. 8-14). Although spacing between adjacent voices occasionally exceeds an octave and voice crossings may occur, the result may be quite striking in context; see for example, the broad sweep of the descending discant and rising alto in this Introit (p. 49, mm. 5-7).

The Sequence in the *Mass for Easter Sunday* in Jena 35 is a very long setting of ten even-numbered verses in a simple homophonic style and contains an unusual number of voice crossings. The Sequences in the *Mass for Whit Monday* and in the *Mass for Feasts of the Blessed Virgin Mary*, on the other hand, are extraordinary settings of this form. The former, for example, is a well-wrought, restrained setting in non-imitative polyphony of five even-numbered verses of equal length. The Sequence in the *Mass for Feasts of the Blessed Virgin Mary* is longer—eight even-numbered verses—and shows several exceptional features. For instance, note the careful attention to the text in verse eight with its extended parallel thirds to the word "sub cultu memoriae" (p. 73, mm. 67-70). Notice the declamatory treatment of "agnum regnantem" (p. 74, mm. 79-81) in the same verse. Declamatory passages are found as well in verse ten. Finally, observe the beginning of verse twelve with its syllabic, homophonic treatment of "audi nos" and a fermata on "nos" (p. 77, mm. 120-121). One might profitably compare such passages to similar ones in Adam Rener's third setting of the Nativity Mass.[19]

Finally, one might compare the Communion in the *Mass for Whit Monday* in this edition with the Communion in the third setting of the *Mass for the Nativity* by Rener.[20] Both are simple, short, and effective settings for this series. On the basis of stylistic consistency and overall quality, it would seem probable that the entire *Mass for Whit Monday*, the Introit in the *Mass for Easter Sunday*, and the Introit, Alleluia, and Sequence in the *Mass for Feasts of the Blessed Virgin Mary* are by Adam Rener.

Performance Practice

The usual voice ranges for the three Mass Proper cycles of this edition are the following: discant, d'-e''; alto, f-a' (descends to e in one movement); tenor, d-g' (ascends to a' in three movements); and bass, G-b (descends to F in two movements). (Pitches are given in Helmholtz pitch notation where middle c = c'.)

The number of singers required for these works may vary depending on practical considerations, but it is important to bear in mind two principles. First, there should be a balance between the choral unison of the plainsong sections and the sections sung in polyphony. Second, the plainsong intonations should be sung by two or three cantors in unison.

If circumstances permit, the following singers should participate: (1) *Cantors*: At least two solo tenors, who sing in unison all the intonations except the intonation for the Gloria, which is sung by one cantor representing the celebrant. (2) *Plainsong choir*: A small ensemble (six to eight) of adult male voices, who sing all the plainsong sections except the intonations, which are sung by the cantors. (3) *Polyphonic choir*: A small ensemble (twelve to sixteen) of mixed voices or of men and boys sings the polyphonic sections.

In a concert performance, it is suggested that the plainsong choir and the polyphonic choir be separated spatially on the stage. This will make the *alternatim* movements, such as the Sequences, most effective in performance. The cantors should be positioned with the plainsong choir.

The method of singing the Introit for all three Mass Proper cycles is as follows. The intonation is sung by two cantors. The rest of the antiphon continues in polyphony. The verse intonation is sung by the two cantors and then the verse is completed

in polyphony. The "Gloria Patri" is begun by the two cantors and completed in choral unison by the plainsong choir, beginning with "Sicut erat." In the *da capo*, the intonation is sung in choral unison by the plainsong choir. The antiphon is then continued by the polyphonic choir, and the movement concludes at "Fine." In the "Gloria Patri" of each Introit and in the Gradual verse "Haec dies," asterisks have been used, as in the *Liber Usualis*, to indicate where the plainsong choir joins the cantors.

In both Masses where it occurs, the Kyrie becomes ninefold with the editorial addition of appropriate plainsong sections from the *Liber Usualis*. It is to be sung *alternatim*, that is, with the invocations sung in choral unison by the plainsong choir alternating with the polyphonic sections. There are no independent passages for the solo cantors in this movement.

Where the Gloria occurs, a solo cantor representing the celebrant sings the opening "Gloria in excelsis Deo." The plainsong choir continues in choral unison with "Et in terra," followed by a regular alternation thereafter of the polyphonic choir and plainsong choir.

The *Mass for Easter Sunday* is the only one in this edition to include a setting of the Gradual; however, only the respond is given in the source. The plainsong verse has been supplied by the editor from the *Liber Usualis* in order to complete the movement. The intonation "Haec dies" is sung by the two cantors. The rest of the respond, beginning with "Quam fecit," is then sung in polyphony. Most of the verse that follows is sung by the two solo cantors. Only toward the very end, at "ejus," does the plainsong choir join in to complete the movement.

The intonation of the Alleluia in the *Mass for Easter Sunday* is sung by the two solo cantors. The remainder of the movement is sung in polyphony. The Alleluia settings in the *Mass for Whit Monday* and in the *Mass for Feasts of the Blessed Virgin Mary* have no plainsong intonations and are sung in polyphony throughout. Since all the Masses are provided with Sequences, the Alleluia respond is not repeated after the verse. Instead, after the verse is completed, the Sequence follows immediately.

In the Sequence, all plainsong sections are sung in choral unison by the plainsong choir. These sections alternate with verses sung by the polyphonic choir.

The Communion is the simplest movement of any in this edition. It is in one section consisting of the antiphon with its intonation. The intonation is sung by the two cantors, after which the movement continues in polyphony to the end.

The Edition

In order to make these works more accessible for study and performance, modern clefs and barring have been used throughout the transcriptions. In the source manuscript, the tenor parts are notated in black non-mensural (chant) notation. In the present edition, the neumes of two or more notes (*podatus, clivis, climacus*, etc.) in the tenor are indicated by slurs, in agreement with the method employed in "modern notation" editions of Gregorian chant. It should be noted, however, that the notation of compound neumes is haphazard in the source, and various interpretations may be possible. The ligatures found in voice parts other than the tenor in the source have been indicated by square brackets placed above the affected notes. Note values are reduced in the ratio of 2:1 ($\downarrow = \downarrow$), and a time signature of 2/2 is given the original *tempus imperfectum diminutum* (¢). All editorial time signatures are enclosed within brackets. Particularly at the ends of sections and movements, a measure of triple meter is sometimes necessary in order to get the final chord to fall on the first beat of a measure. Following the initial meter signature of each Mass Proper cycle, such signatures are repeated in this edition only when necessary for meter restoration following an editorial or source change in meter. Unless otherwise indicated, the value of the half-note is constant through all meter changes.

Spelling, punctuation, hyphenation, and capitalization of the text have been modernized for ease of performance. Any other textual deviation from the source has been enclosed within brackets in the edition. In the matter of text underlay, the voice bearing the *cantus firmus* presents very few problems; only rarely must a compound neume be divided in order to accommodate two syllables. However, in the other voices, text placement is often haphazard in the source, and the editor has had to establish some principles of text underlay. In choral music of this period, forcing the text to agree with the musical structure by shifting individual syllables a great distance in the phrase is not appropriate. On the contrary, it would seem better to follow as closely as is practicable the text underlay given in the source. In brief, syllables have been underlaid in the transcription to their nearest significant notes, that is, to notes of longer value, to notes on strong beats, or to notes occupying more important structural parts of the phrase. This procedure is one that could have been applied by sixteenth-century singers, with two or three singers on a part, and that, moreover, avoids the objectionable course of placing a new syllable under the middle of a group of semiminims, as occurs occasionally in the manuscript. In doubtful cases, the prescriptions of Zarlino have been kept in mind.[21]

Jena 35 includes plainsong only for intonations for the Introit antiphons and their verses and for the intonations preceding each Communion and the Gradual *Haec dies*. However, the Tones for the "Gloria Patri" at the Introit are not given in the manuscript, and although the Kyries, Glorias, and Sequences are *alternatim* movements, they are represented in Jena 35 only by their polyphonic sections. Therefore, the editor has had to supply both text and music for all of the missing plainsong in order to make a complete and meaningful performance possible. Since the polyphonic sections of the source invariably employ the strict *cantus firmus* technique, and since these sections generally show only insignificant variants when compared to the melodies as given in modern chant books, the editor has used the *Liber Usualis* as a source for the added plainsong in the present transcription. The Sequences *Laudes Salvatori* and *Ave praeclara maris stella*, however, are no longer in use and, therefore, not found in the *Liber Usualis*. The plainsong supplied for these two Sequences is taken from Schubiger.[22] All of the editorially added plainsong is enclosed in square brackets; where necessary, it has been transposed in order to agree with the polyphonic setting. The asterisk is used, as in the *Liber Usualis*, to mark the places where the plainsong choir joins the cantors.

In plainsong settings using the strict *cantus firmus* technique, an overly zealous approach in the matter of adding editorial accidentals is especially unwise. For example, in the Gloria in the *Mass for Easter Sunday*, the alternating sections of plainsong and polyphony are sometimes quite short. If one attempts systematically to provide leading tones wherever possible and to raise all thirds in final chords, there will be a rapid alternation between plainsong modal sections and pseudo-major/minor polyphonic sections. This effect is foreign to the style of sacred polyphony in the early sixteenth century and not necessarily musical to modern ears.

Accordingly, caution has been exercised in the use of editorial accidentals, and the following principles have been applied: (1) in important structural cadences, the *subsemitonium* has been provided, when necessary, by means of an editorial accidental above the staff; (2) B has been flatted when it is an upper neighbor; (3) B has been flatted when it is approached or left by a leap; (4) in a transposed mode, the principles of flatting B apply to flatting E; (5) the tritone is always avoided when it occurs in a direct leap, and it is usually avoided when it is outlined in the melodic design; (6) the leading tone is not raised in a Phrygian cadence; (7) *musica ficta* is ordinarily not applied within a phrase when to do so would result in an augmented or diminished harmonic interval; (8) the third in a final chord is usually raised to provide a major triad.

Most of the exceptions to these principles fall into one of three categories: either the chromatic inflection of a note creates a new problem, such as a harmonic tritone; or the note to be inflected is doubled in another voice; or the note is found in the tenor, where to apply an editorial accidental would be completely foreign to the conservative respect for the integrity of the plainsong *cantus firmus* shown by Adam Rener and his colleagues in these strict *cantus firmus* settings.

Critical Notes

The Critical Notes indicate the location of each work within the primary source, Jena 35. Roediger's thematic index numbers for the Jena choirbooks (*Die geistlichen Musikhandschriften*, II: Notenverzeichnis) are also provided, along with the location of the *cantus firmus* in the *Liber Usualis* (No. 801 Tournai: Desclée, 1956; referred to hereafter as LU) or in Schubiger, *Die Sängerschule St. Gallens*. The very few manuscript errors are cited below. L = long, Br = breve, SB = semibreve, Mi = minim. There are no known concordances for these Mass Proper cycles.

Mass for Easter Sunday

Introit—Jena 35: 6v-8 (Jena 478), LU 777; "Gloria Patri" (Tone 4): LU 15.

Kyrie—Jena 35: 8v-9 (Jena 479), LU 16 (Mass I). The source spelling of "eleyson" has been retained throughout this edition, since only one note has been provided for the second syllable in the manuscript. In the plainsong, the movement has the following form: *aaa bbb ccd*.

Gloria—Jena 35: 8v-11 (Jena 479), LU 16-18 (Mass I).

Gradual—Jena 35: 11v-13 (Jena 480), LU 778. After the verse, the polyphonic respond may be repeated (see LU, p. xv). M. 43, alto, note 1 is a Mi. M. 44, discant, note 1 is a Br.

Alleluia—Jena 35: 12v-14 (Jena 481), LU 779. In the source, the final melisma of the Alleluia verse is omitted from the *cantus firmus* setting.

Sequence—Jena 35: 14v-19 (Jena 482), Schubiger 11. In verses 14 and 15, the *cantus firmus* is trans-

posed up a fifth from the pitch level given in Schubiger.

Communion—Jena 35: 19v-20 (Jena 483), LU 781.

Mass for Whit Monday

Introit—Jena 35: 46v-48 (Jena 499), LU 887; "Gloria Patri" (Tone 2): LU 14.

Alleluia—Jena 35: 47v-50 (Jena 500), LU 880. The source has a fermata in all voices at the end of the first phrase to indicate that the singers should return to the beginning and repeat the opening phrase.

Sequence—Jena 35: 50v-52 (Jena 501), LU 880.

Communion—Jena 35: 52v-53 (Jena 502), LU 889.

Mass for Feasts of the Blessed Virgin Mary

Introit—Jena 35: 62v-64 (Jena 508), LU 1263; "Gloria Patri" (Tone 2): LU 14. Outside Paschal Time, the final "alleluia" of the antiphon is omitted. The *signum congruentiae* in the alto in m. 36 and in the remaining voices in m. 37 indicates the final cadence of the antiphon for use outside Paschal Time. The verse, "Sentiat omnes," is no longer in use. M. 16, discant, notes 5 and 6 are Mi Mi. M. 49, discant, note 3 to m. 50, note 1, illegible in manuscript.

Kyrie—Jena 35: 64v-65 (Jena 509), LU 40 (Mass IX). The plainsong model has the form *aba cdc efe'*.

Gloria—Jena 35: 65v-68 (Jena 509), LU 40-42.

Alleluia—Jena 35: 68v-70 (Jena 510), LU 1267. The fermata in all voices over the last syllable of the word "alleluia" indicates the point at which the singers return to the beginning to repeat the opening phrase. M. 38, bass, note 1 is a Br.

Sequence—Jena 35: 70v-75 (Jena 511), Schubiger 56.

Communion—Jena 35: 75v-76 (Jena 512), LU 1268.

Acknowledgments

Grateful acknowledgment is made to Georg Olms Verlag, Hildesheim, for permission to quote from their reprint of the book by Anselm Schubiger, *Die Sängerschule St. Gallens*; to the Abbey of St. Andrew, Bruges, for permission to reprint texts for the *Saint Andrew Daily Missal*; to Deutsches Musikgeschichtliches Archiv for a photocopy of Jena 35; to Dr. Judith Schomber for translation of those texts no longer in current use; and to the Georgia Southern College Research Committee (Dr. Lawrence Huff, Chairman) for several research grants.

Robert E. Gerken
Statesboro, Georgia

April 1982

Notes

1. See Robert E. Gerken, "The Polyphonic Cycles of the Proper of the Mass in the Trent Codex 88 and Jena Choirbooks 30 and 35" (Ph.D. diss., Indiana University, 1969).

2. *Die Musik in Geschichte und Gegenwart*, s.v. "Jenaer Musikhandschriften," by Lothar Hoffmann-Erbrecht.

3. Ibid.

4. Karl Erich Roediger, *Die geistlichen Musikhandschriften der Universitäts-Bibliothek Jena* (Jena: Frommannsche Buchhandlung, 1935), Vol. I: Text; Vol. II: Notenverzeichnis.

5. Ibid., I:3.

6. Ibid., I:12.

7. Ibid., I:21.

8. See Robert Leroy Parker, "The Motets of Adam Rener (ca. 1485-ca. 1520)" (Ph.D. diss., University of Texas, 1963).

9. Ibid., pp. 1 ff. and Appendix A.

10. See *Die Musik in Geschichte und Gegenwart*, s.v. "Rener(us) Leodiensis," by Jürgen Kindermann.

11. Parker, "The Motets," pp. 180 ff., describes these methods.

12. Kindermann, "Rener(us)."

13. Ibid.

14. Ibid.

15. Roediger, *Die geistlichen Musikhandschriften*, I: 84, describes liturgical music at pre-Reformation Wittenberg.

16. Ibid. The rules are described.

17. See David A. Sutherland, ed., *The Lyons Contrapunctus*, Recent Researches in the Music of the Renaissance, vols. 21, 22 (Madison, Wisconsin: A-R Editions, 1976).

18. Anselm Schubiger, *Die Sängerschule St. Gallens vom 8. bis 12. Jahrhundert* (1858; reprint ed., Hildesheim: Georg Olms Verlagsbuchhandlung, 1966).

19. Parker, "The Motets," pp. 283 ff.

20. Ibid., pp. 292 ff.

21. Zarlino, *Istitutioni armoniche* (Venice, 1558), Bk. IV, ch. 33.

22. Schubiger, *Die Sängerschule*.

Texts and Translations

The texts of the Sequences in the *Mass for Easter Sunday* and in the *Mass for Feasts of the Blessed Virgin Mary* and the tropes of the Gloria in the *Mass for Feasts of the Blessed Virgin Mary* were translated by Dr. Judith Schomber, Department of Foreign Languages, Georgia Southern College. The remaining translations were taken from *The Saint Andrew Daily Missal*, Dom Gaspar Lefebvre, O.S.B. The Ordinary texts (except for the troped Gloria) and the text of the *Gloria Patri* have not been translated.

Mass for Easter Sunday

Introit

Resurrexi, Et adhuc tecum sum, alleluia: posuisti super me manum tuam, alleluia: mirabilis facta est scientia tua, alleluia, alleluia. *Verse.* Domine, probasti me, et cognovisti me: Tu cognovisti sessionem meam, et resurrectionem meam. *Gloria Patri.*

Introit

I arose, and am still with Thee, alleluia: Thou hast laid Thine hand upon me, alleluia: Thy knowledge is become wonderful, alleluia, alleluia. *Verse.* Lord, Thou hast searched me, and known me: Thou knowest my sitting down and my rising up. *Gloria Patri.*

Gradual

Haec dies, Quam fecit Dominus: exsultemus, et laetemur in ea. *Verse.* Confitemini Domino, quoniam bonus: quoniam in saeculum misericordia ejus.

Gradual

This is the day which the Lord hath made: let us rejoice and be glad in it. *Verse.* Give praise unto the Lord, for He is good: for His mercy endureth for ever.

Alleluia

Verse. Pascha nostrum immolatus est Christus.

Alleluia

Verse. Christ our Pasch is sacrificed.

Sequence

1. Laudes Salvatori voce modulemur supplici. 2. Et devotis melodiis caelesti Domino jubilemus Messiae. 3. Qui se ipsum exinanivit ut nos perditos liberaret homines: 4. Carne gloriam deitatis occulens. Pannis tegitur in praesepi miserans praecepti transgressorem, pulsum patria, paradisi nudulum. 5. Joseph, Mariae, Simeoni subditur. Circumciditur et legali hostia mundatur ut peccator, nostra qui solet relaxare crimina. 6. Servi subiit manus baptizandus et perfert fraudes temptatoris, fugit persequentum lapides. 7. Fames patitur, dormit et tristatur ac lavat discipulis pedes, deus homo, summus humilis. 8. Sed tamen inter haec abjecta corporis, ejus deitas nequaquam quivit latere, signis variis et doctrinis prodita. 9. Aquam nuptiis dat saporis vinei, caecos oculos claro lumine vestivit, lepram luridam tactu fugat placido. 10. Putres suscitat mortuos membraque curat debilia. Fluxus sanguinis constrinxit et saturavit quinque de panibus quinque millia. 11. Stagnum peragrat fluctuans ceu siccum littus, ven-

Sequence

1. Let us sing praises to the Savior with suppliant voice. 2. And with pious hymns let us rejoice in the heavenly Lord, the Messiah, 3. He who emptied Himself to us lost men: 4. Hiding the glory of divinity in flesh. He who takes compassion on the transgressor of the commandment who was banished from his home and deprived of paradise, is swaddled in the manger. 5. He is subject to Joseph, Mary, and Simeon. He who is wont to forgive our sins is, like a sinner, circumcised and purified by sacrifice in accordance with the law. 6. He submitted to the servant's hands for baptism, and He endures the deceits of the Temptor and flees the stones of the persecutors. 7. God and Man, exalted and humble, suffers hunger, is weary and troubled, and washes the disciples' feet. 8. But still, despite these base afflictions of the body, His divinity could by no means be concealed and was made manifest in diverse signs and teachings. 9. He gives water with the taste of wine at a wedding, He clothed blind

tus sedat. Linguam reserat constrictam, reclusit aures privatas vocibus, febres depulit. 12. Post haec mira miracula taliaque, 13. Sponte sua comprenditur et damnatur, 14. Et se crucifigi non despexit. 15. Sed sol ejus mortem non aspexit. 16. Illuxit dies, quem fecit Dominus, mortem devastans et victor suis apparens dilectoribus vivus, 17. Primo Mariae, dehinc Apostolis, docens scripturas, cor aperiens ut clausa de ipso reserarent. 18. Favent igitur resurgenti Christo cuncta gaudiis: Flores, segetes redivivo fructu vernant, et volucres, gelu tristi terso, dulce jubilant. 19. Lucent clarius sol et luna, morte Christi turbida. Tellus herbida resurgenti plaudit Christo, quae tremula ejus morte se casuram minitat. 20. Ergo die ista exsultemus, qua nobis viam vitae resurgens patefecit Jesus. 21. Astra, solum, mare jucundentur, et cuncti gratulentur in caelis spiritales chori tonanti.

eyes in dazzling light, He drives away ghastly leprosy with a gentle touch. 10. He raises the rotting dead and cures weak limbs. He stopped the flow of blood, and He filled five thousand with five loaves of bread. 11. He traverses the billowing waves as though it were dry shore, He calms the winds. He unlocks the fettered tongue, He opens ears deprived of voices, He drove out fevers. 12. After all these wonderful and remarkable miracles, 13. By His will He is seized and condemned, 14. And He did not disdain that He Himself be crucified. 15. But the sun did not behold His death. 16. The day dawned which the Lord made which destroyed death; he appeared alive to His own beloved. 17. First to Mary, then to the Apostles, teaching scriptures, opening their hearts that they might, through him, open what had been barred. 18. Therefore all things extol the risen Christ with rejoicing: flowers, and fields flourish with fruit reborn, and birds, after the gloomy frost is thawed, sweetly rejoice. 19. The sun and the moon, obscured by the death of Christ, shine more brightly. The grassy earth, which quaked and threatened to perish at His death, rejoices in the risen Christ. 20. Therefore let us rejoice on this day, wherein the risen Jesus has laid open the way of life for us. 21. Let the stars, the sun, the sea be glad, and let all the choruses of spirits in heaven honor the Thunderer.

Communion

Pascha nostrum Immolatus est Christus, alleluia: itaque epulemur in azymis sinceritatis et veritatis, alleluia, alleluia, alleluia.

Communion

Christ our Pasch is immolated, alleluia: therefore let us feast with the unleavened bread of sincerity and truth, alleluia, alleluia, alleluia.

Mass for Whit Monday

Introit

Cibavit eos Ex adipe frumenti, alleluia: et de petra, melle saturavit eos, alleluia, alleluia. *Verse.* Exsultate Deo adjutori nostro: Jubilate Deo Jacob. *Gloria Patri.*

Introit

He fed them with the finest of wheat, alleluia: and filled them with honey out of the rock, alleluia, alleluia. *Verse.* Rejoice to God our helper: sing aloud to the God of Jacob. *Gloria Patri.*

Alleluia

Verse. Veni Sancte Spiritus, reple tuorum corda fidelium: et tui amoris in eis ignem accende.

Alleluia

Verse. Come, Holy Spirit, fill the hearts of Thy faithful: and kindle in them the fire of Thy love.

Sequence

Veni Sancte Spiritus, Et emitte caelitus Lucis tuae radium. 2. Veni pater pauperum, Veni dator munerum, Veni lumen cordium. 3. Consolator optime, Dulcis hospes animae, Dulce refrigerium. 4. In labore requies, In aestu temperies, in fletu solatium. 5. O lux beatissima, Reple cordis intima

Sequence

Come, Holy Ghost, send down those beams, Which sweetly flow in silent streams From Thy bright throne above. 2. O, come, Thou Father of the poor, O, come, Thou source of all our store, Come fill our hearts with love. 3. O Thou of comforters the best, O Thou the soul's delightful guest, The pil-

Tuorum fidelium. 6. Sine tuo numine, Nihil est in homine, Nihil est innoxium. 7. Lava quod est sordidum, Riga quod est aridum, Sana quod est saucium. 8. Flecte quod est rigidum, Fove quod est frigidum, Rege quod est devium. 9. Da tuis fidelibus, In te confidentibus, Sacrum septenarium. 10. Da virtutis meritum, Da salutis exitum, Da perenne gaudium.

grim's sweet relief. 4. Rest art Thou in our toil, most sweet Refreshment in the noonday heat, And solace in our grief. 5. O blessed Light of Life Thou art, Fill with Thy Light the inmost hearts Of those that hope in Thee. 6. Without Thy Godhead nothing can Have any price or worth in man, Nothing can harmless be. 7. Lord, wash our sinful stains away, Water from heaven our barren clay, Our wounds and bruises heal. 8. To Thy sweet yoke our stiff necks bow, Warm with Thy love our hearts of snow, Our wandering feet recall. 9. Grant to Thy faithful, dearest Lord, Whose only hope is in Thy Word, Thy sevenfold gift of grace. 10. Grant us in life Thy grace that we In peace may die and ever be In joy before Thy face.

Communion

Spiritus Sanctus Docebit vos, alleluia: quaecumque dixero vobis, alleluia, alleluia.

Communion

The Holy Ghost will teach you, alleluia, whatsoever I shall have said to you, alleluia, alleluia.

Mass for Feasts of the Blessed Virgin Mary

Introit

Salve Sancta Parens, enixa puerpera Regem, qui caelum terramque regit in saecula saeculorum, alleluia. *Verse.* Sentiat omnes tuum levamen: Quicumque celebrant tuam commemorationem. *Gloria Patri.*

Introit

Hail, holy Mother, thou who didst bring forth the King who ruleth heaven and earth for ever and ever, alleluia. *Verse.* Let all men whatsoever who celebrate thy feast feel thy solace. *Gloria Patri.*

Gloria

Domine Fili unigenite, Jesu Christe. Spiritus et alme orphanorum paraclite. Domine Deus, Agnus Dei, Filius Patris. Primogenitus Marie virginis Matris. Qui tollis peccata mundi . . . suscipe deprecationem nostram. Ad Mariae gloriam. Qui sedes ad dexteram Patris . . . Quoniam tu solus sanctus, Mariam sanctificans. Tu solus Dominus. Tu solus Altissimus, Mariam coronans, Jesu Christe. Cum Sancto Spiritu, in gloria Dei Patris. Amen.

Gloria

O Lord Jesus Christ, the only-begotten Son. Breath and kind advocate of orphans. O Lord God, Lamb of God, Son of the Father. First-born son of the Virgin Mother Mary. You who take away the sins of the world . . . Give ear to our prayer. To the glory of Mary. You who sit at the right hand of the Father . . . For you only art holy, sanctifying Mary. You only are the Lord. You alone are high above all, crowning Mary, Jesus Christ. With the Holy Spirit, In the glory of God the Father. Amen.

Alleluia.

Verse. Virga Jesse floruit: Virgo Deum et hominem genuit: pacem Deus reddidit, in se reconcilians ima summis.

Alleluia.

Verse. The rod of Jesse hath blossomed: a virgin hath brought forth God and man: God hath restored peace, reconciling in Himself the lowest with the highest.

Sequence

1. Ave praeclara maris stella, in lucem gentium, Maria, divinitus orta. 2. Euge Dei porta, quae non aperta, veritatis lumen ipsum solem justitiae indutum carne, ducis in orbem. 3. Virgo decus mundi, regina coeli, praeelecta ut sol, pulchra lunaris ut fulgor, agnosce omnes te diligentes. 4. Te plenam

Sequence

1. Hail, magnificent star of the sea, Mary, risen by divine power to be the light of the world. 2. Hail, portal of God, who, unopened, guide into the world, clothed in flesh, the Light of truth, the very Sun of justice. 3. Virgin, glory of the world, queen of heaven, preferred as the sun, beautiful as the

fide virgam almae stirpis Jesse nascituram priores desideraverunt patres et Prophetae. 5. Te lignum vitae sancto rorante pneumate parituram divini floris amygdalum signavit Gabriel. 6. Tu agnum regem, terrae dominatorem, moabitici de petra deserti ad montem filiae Sion transduxisti. 7. Tuque furentem Leviathan serpentem tortuosumque, et vecten collidens damnoso crimine mundum exemisti. 8. Hinc gentium nos reliquiae, tuae sub cultu memoriae, mirum in modum quem es enixa propitiationis agnum regnantem coelo aeternaliter devocamus ad aram mactandum misterialiter. 9. Hinc manna verum Israelitis veris, veri Abrahae filiis, admirantibus quondam, Moysi quem typus figurabat, jam nunc abducto velo datur prospici; ora Virgo, nos illo pane coeli dignos effici. 10. Fac fontem dulcem, quem in deserto petra praemonstravit, degustare cum sincera fide, renesque constringi, lotos in mari anguem aeneum in cruce speculari. 11. Fac igni sancto, patrisque verbo, quod rubus ut flamma tu portasti, Virgo Mater facta, pecuali pelle, distinctos pede, mundis labiis, cordeque propinquare. 12. Audi nos, nam te filius nihil negans honorat. 13. Salva nos, Jesu, pro quibus Virgo Mater te orat. 14. Da fontem boni visere, da puros mentis oculos in te defigere. 15. Quo hausto sapientiae saporem vitae valeat mens intelligere; 16. Christianismi fidem operibus redimere, beatoque fine ex hujus incolatu, saeculi auctor, ad te transire.

splendor of the moon, acknowledge all who love you. 4. The patriarchs and prophets of old longed for you to be born, full of faith, the rod of the fair stock of Jesse. 5. Gabriel revealed that you were to give birth to the tree of life, the tree of the divine flower, when bedewed by the Holy Spirit. 6. You have led the Lamb, the King, the Ruler of the earth, from the rock of the Moab desert to the mountains of the daughter of Sion. 7. You have destroyed the mad Leviathan, twisted and writhing, whose fangs envenom the world with damnable sin. 8. Therefore, we, the remnants of the peoples, in the cult of your memory, call down Him whom you bore miraculously as the Lamb of Atonement, who reigns forever in heaven, to the altar for the mystery of sacrifice. 9. Therefore the true manna is now given to be beheld with the veil removed to the true Israelites, sons of true Abraham, who long ago adored Him whom the prototype of Moses prefigured: pray, Virgin, that we be made worthy of heaven by that bread. 10. Make us taste with sincere faith the sweet fountain that the rock prefigured in the desert, and make us gird our loins and, when washed in the sea, behold the bronze serpent on the cross. 11. Let us approach the sacred fire, the word of the Father, which you bore as the bush in flames bore it, o Virgin made mother, with smooth skins, adorned in foot and with clean lips and heart. 12. Hear us, for the Son honors you, denying you nothing. 13. Save us, O Jesus, on behalf of whom the Virgin Mother prays to You. 14. Grant that we may behold a fountain of goodness, grant that we may fix pure contemplation on you. 15. This having been drunk, may the mind be able to understand the taste of the knowledge of life; 16. To adorn the faith of Christianity by works, and at the blessed end, to pass over to you, creator of the world, from its dwelling within it.

Communion

Beata viscera Mariae Virginis, quae portaverunt aeterni Patris Filium. Alleluia, alleluia.

Communion

Blessed is the womb of the Virgin Mary, which bore the Son of the Eternal Father. Alleluia, alleluia.

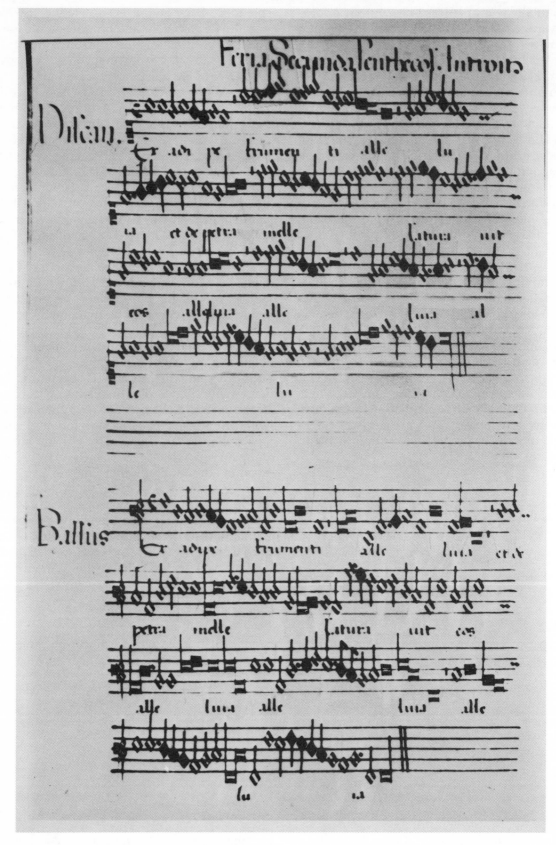

Plate I. *Mass for Whit Monday*. Introit *Cibavit*, discant and bass. Jena 35, fol. 46v.

Plate II. *Mass for Whit Monday*. Introit *Cibavit*, alto and tenor. Jena 35, fol. 47.

THREE MASS PROPER CYCLES
FROM JENA 35

Mass for Easter Sunday

Introit *Resurrexi*

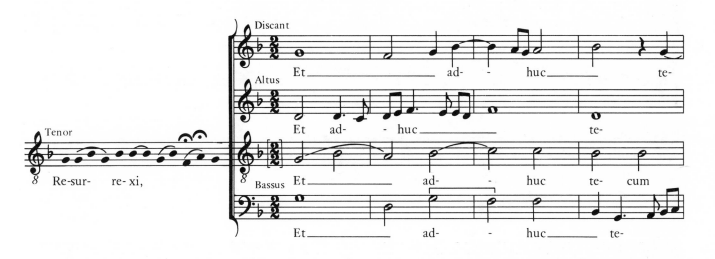

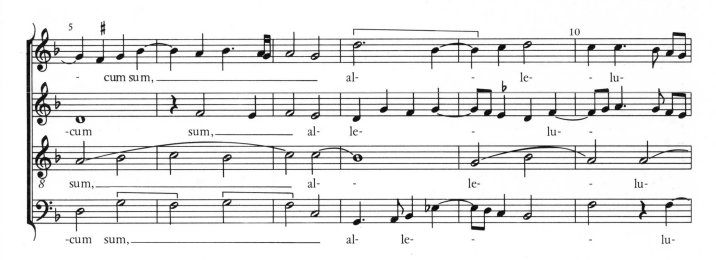

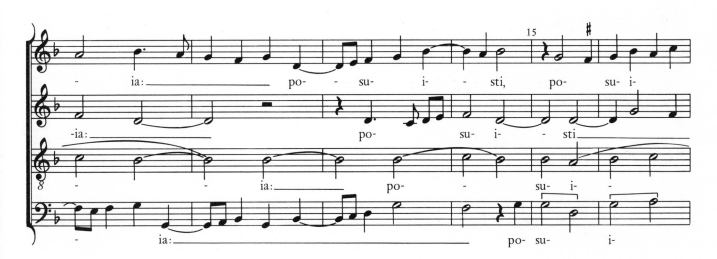

2

4

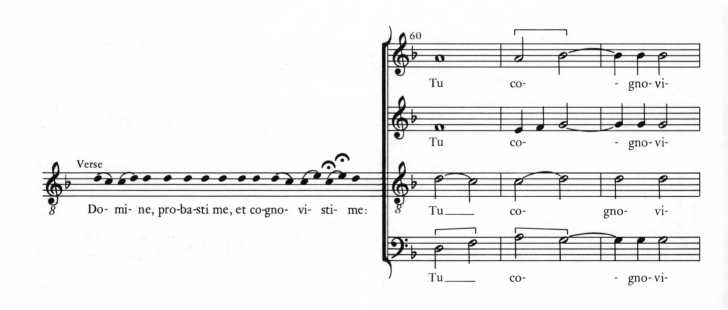

Verse

Do- mi- ne, pro-ba-sti me, et co-gno- vi- sti- me:

Tu co- - gno- vi-

Tu co- - gno- vi-

Tu_____ co- gno- vi-

Tu_____ co- - gno- vi-

-sti ses- si- o - nem me- am,_____

-sti ses- si- o- nem_____ me - am,

-sti ses- si- o- nem me - am,

-sti ses- si- o- nem_____ me - am,_____

et re- sur- re- cti- o- - nem_ me - am.

et re- sur- re- cti- o- nem me - am.

et re- sur- re- cti- o- - nem_____ me- am.

et re- sur- re- cti- o- nem_____ me - am.

Glo- ri- a Pa- tri, et Fi- li- o, et Spi- ri- tu- i San- cto, *Sic- ut e- rat

[D. C. al Fine]

in prin- ci- pi- o, et nunc, et sem- per, et in sae- cu- la sae- cu- lo- rum. A-men.

6

Kyrie

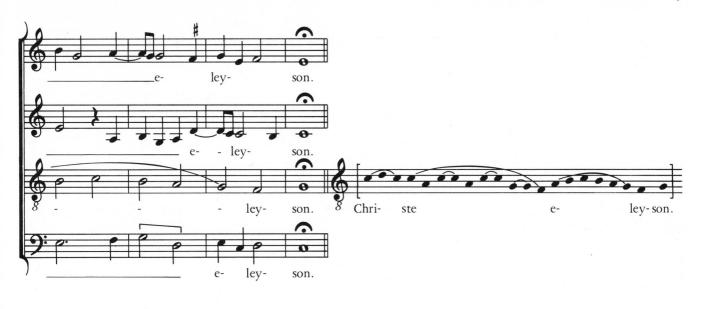

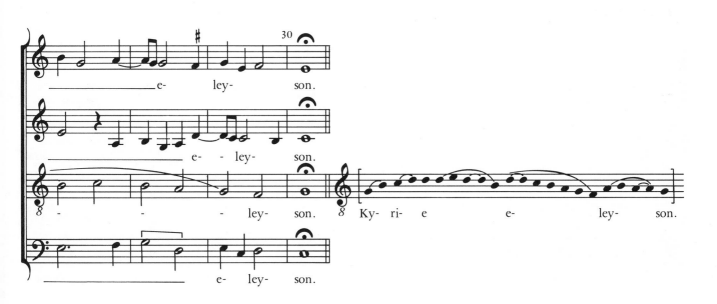

8

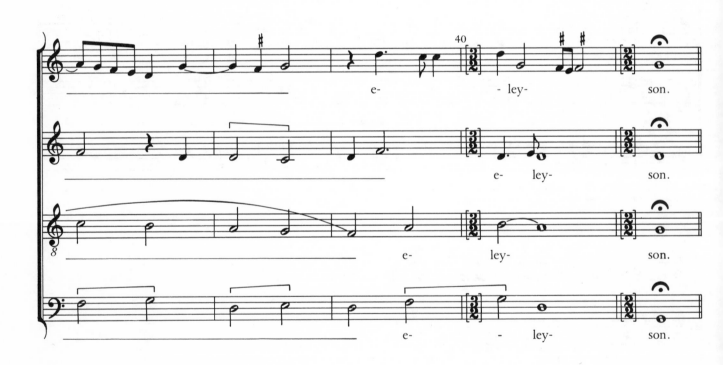

Gloria

10

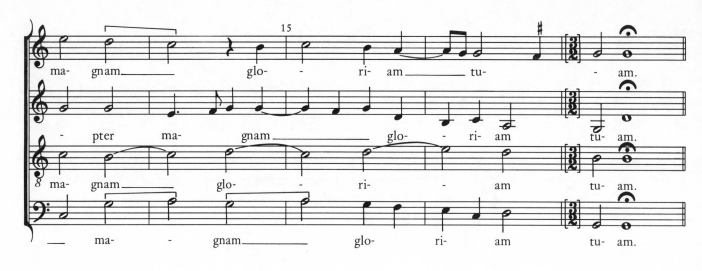

ma- gnam_____ glo- ri- am_____ tu- am.

_pter ma- gnam_____ gno- ri- am tu- am.

ma- gnam_____ glo- ri- am tu- am.

__ ma - gnam_____ glo- ri- am tu- am.

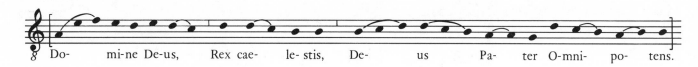

Do- mi- ne De-us, Rex cae- le- stis, De- us Pa- ter O-mni- po- tens.

Do- mi - ne_____ Fi- li_____ u- ni- ge- ni- te

Do- mi - ne Fi- li_____ u- ni- ge- ni- te

Do- mi - ne Fi- li_____ u- ni- ge- ni- te

Do- mi - ne Fi - li u- ni- ge- ni- te

Je- - su_____ Chri- ste.

Je- su_____ Chri- ste.

Je- - su_____ Chri- ste. Do- mi- ne De-us, A- gnus De- i,

Je- - su_____ Chri- ste.

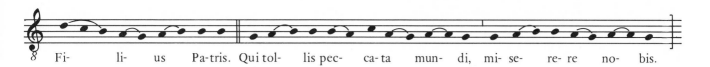

Fi- li- us Pa- tris. Qui tol- lis pec- ca- ta mun- di, mi- se- re- re no- bis.

Qui tol- lis pec- ca- ta mun- di,

Qui tol- lis pec- ca- ta mun- di,

Qui tol- lis pec- ca- ta mun- di,

Qui tol- lis pec- ca- ta mun- di,

sus- ci- pe de- pre- ca- ti- o- nem no- stram.

sus- ci- pe de- pre- ca- ti- o- nem no- stram.

sus- ci- pe de- pre- ca- ti- o- nem no- stram.

sus- ci- pe de- pre- ca- ti- o- nem no- stram.

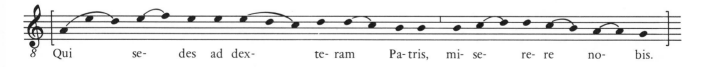

Qui se- des ad dex- te- ram Pa- tris, mi- se- re- re no- bis.

Gradual *Haec dies*

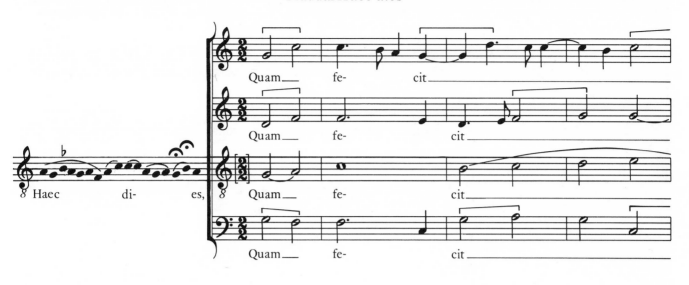

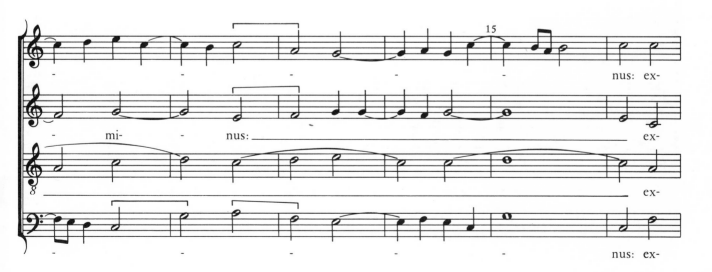

14

Alleluia *Pascha nostrum*

18

tus_____ est_____ Chri-

- - - - - tus_____

- - tus_____

- - - - - tus

-stus._____

est Chri- -stus._____

____ est Chri- - - -stus._____

est_____ Chri- stus._____

Sequence *Laudes Salvatori*

2. Et de- vo- tis me- lo-

2. Et de- vo- tis me- lo-

1. Lau-des Sal- va- to- ri vo- ce mo- du- le- mur sup-pli- ci.

2. Et de- vo- tis me- lo-

2. Et de- vo- tis me- lo-

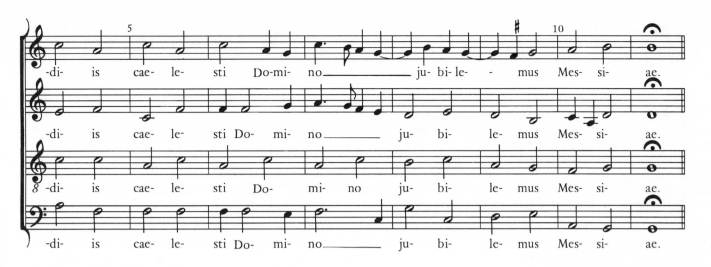

-di- is cae-le- sti Do-mi- no_____ ju-bi- le- - mus Mes- si- ae.

-di- is cae-le- sti Do- mi- no_____ ju- bi- le- mus Mes- si- ae.

-di- is cae-le- sti Do- mi- no ju- bi- le- mus Mes- si- ae.

-di- is cae-le- sti Do- mi- no_____ ju- bi- le- mus Mes- si- ae.

3. Qui se i- psum ex- i- na- ni- vit ut nos per- di- tos li- be- ra- ret ho- mi- nes:

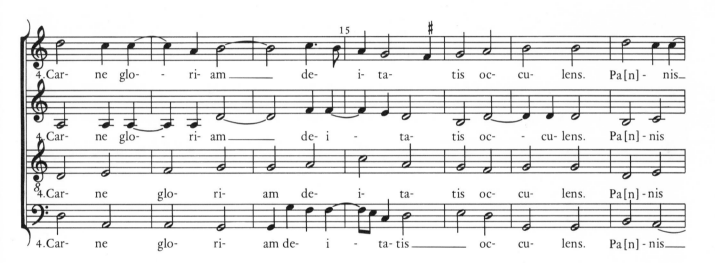

4.Car- ne glo- ri- am_____ de- i- ta- tis oc- cu- lens. Pa[n]- nis___

4.Car- ne glo- ri- am_____ de- i- ta- tis oc- cu- lens. Pa[n]- nis

4.Car- ne glo- ri- am de- i- ta- tis oc- cu- lens. Pa[n]- nis

4.Car- ne glo- ri- am de- i- ta- tis_____ oc- cu- lens. Pa[n]- nis___

__te- gi- tur in___ prae- se- pi mi- se- rans prae- ce- pti_____trans-

te- gi- tur in prae- - se- pi___ mi- se- rans prae- ce- pti trans-

te- gi- tur in prae- se- pi mi- se- rans prae- ce- pti trans-

__te- gi- tur in___ prae- - se- pi mi- se- rans prae- ce- pti trans-

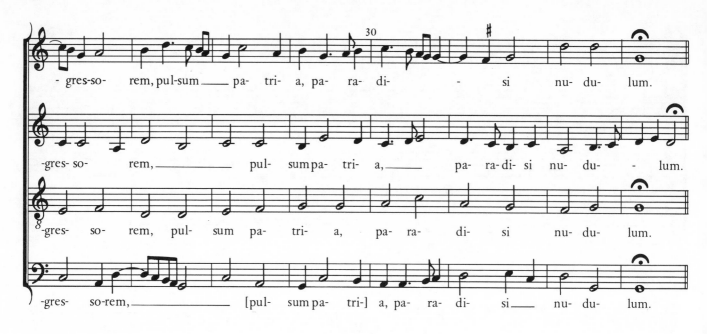

-gres-so- rem, pul-sum____ pa- tri- a, pa- ra- di- si nu- du- lum.

-gres- so- rem,_____ pul- sum pa- tri- a,____ pa- ra- di- si nu du- lum.

-gres- so- rem, pul- sum pa- tri- a, pa- ra- di- si nu- du- lum.

-gres- so- rem,_____ [pul- sum pa- tri-] a, pa- ra- di- si____ nu- du- lum.

5. Jo- seph, Ma- ri- ae, Si- me- o- ni sub- di- tur. Cir- cum- ci- di- tur et le- ga- li

ho- sti- a mun- da- tur ut pec- ca- tor, no- stra qui so- let re- la- xa- re cri- mi- na.

6. Ser- vi su- bi- it ma- nus____ ba- pti- -zan- dus____ et per- fert frau-

6. Ser- vi____ su- bi- it ma- nus ba- pti- zan- dus et____ per- fert

6. Ser- vi su- bi- it ma- nus ba- pti- zan- dus et per- fert

6. Ser- vi su- bi- it ma- nus ba- pti- zan- dus et per- fert

des tem-pta-to- ris, fu-git per-se-quen- -tum la- pi-des.

frau-des tem-pta-to- ris, fu-git per- se- quen-tum la- pi-des.

frau-des tem-pta- to-ris, fu-git per-se- quen-tum la- pi-des.

frau-des tem-pta- to-ris, fu-git per-se- quen-tum la- pi-des.

7. Fa-mes pa-ti-tur, dor-mit et tri-sta-tur ac la-vat di-sci-pu-lis pe-des, de-us ho-mo,

8. Sed ta- men in- ter haec ab- je-

8. Sed ta- men in- ter haec ab- je-

sum-mus hu-mi-lis.

8. Sed ta- men in- ter haec ab- je-

8. Sed ta- men in- ter haec ab- je-cta

-cta cor- po- ris, e- jus de-i- tas ne-qua-

-cta cor- -po-ris, e- jus de- i-tas ne- -qua-

-cta cor- po-ris, e- jus de- i-tas ne-

cor- po- ris, e- jus de-i- tas ne-

-quam___ qui- vit la- te- re, si- gnis va- ri- is

-quam___ qui- vit___ la- te- re, si- gnis va- ri- is

-qua- quam qui- vit la- te- re, si- gnis va- ri- is

-qua- quam qui- vit la- te- re, si- gnis va- ri- is

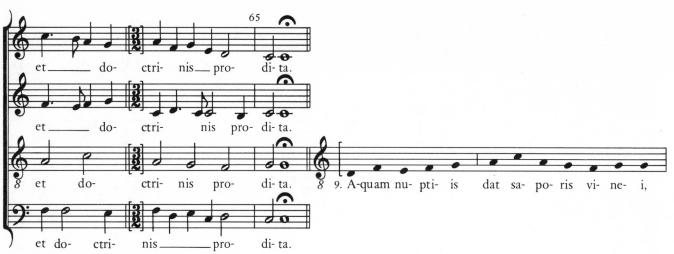

et___ do- ctri- nis___ pro- di- ta.

et___ do- ctri- nis pro- di- ta.

et do- ctri- nis pro- di- ta.

9. A-quam nu- pti- is dat sa- po- ris vi- ne- i,

et do- ctri- nis___ pro- di- ta.

cae- cos o- cu- los cla- ro lu- mi- ne ve- sti- vit, le- pram lu- ri- dam ta- ctu fu- gat pla- ci- do.

10. Pu- tres sus- ci- tat mor- - tu- os mem- bra- que___ cu-

10. Pu- tres sus- ci- tat___ mor- tu- os mem- bra- que cu-

10. Pu- tres sus- ci- tat mor- tu- os mem- bra- que cu-

10. Pu- tres sus- ci- tat mor- - tu- os mem- bra- que___ cu-

-rat ___ de- bi- li- a. ___ Flu- xus san- gui- nis con- strin-

-rat de- bi - li- a. Flu- xus san- gui- nis con- strin-

-rat de- bi - li - a. Flu- xus san- gui- nis con- strin-

- rat de- bi - li - a. Flu- xus san- gui- nis con- strin-

-xit ___ et ___ sa- tu- - ra- vit ___ quin- que ___ de pa- ni- bus ___

-xit ___ et ___ sa- tu- ra- vit quin- que de ___ pa- ni- bus ___

-xit et sa- - tu- ra- vit quin- que de pa- ni- bus

-xit ___ et ___ sa- tu- ra- vit quin- que ___ de pa- ni- bus ___

quin- que mil- - li- a.

quin- que ___ mil- li- a.

quin- que mil- - li- a. 11. Sta- gnum pe- ra- grat flu- ctu- ans ceu sic- cum lit- tus,

___ quin- que mil- - li- a.

ven- tus se- dat. Lin- guam re- se- rat con- stri- ctam, re- clu- sit au- res pri- va- tas vo- ci- bus, fe- bres de- pu- lit.

26

Domi- nus, mor- tem de- va- stans et vi- ctor ____ su- is ap- pa-

Domi- nus, mor- tem de- va- stans et vi- ctor su- is ap-

Domi- nus, mor- tem de- va- stans et vi- ctor su- is ap-

Domi- nus, mor- tem de- va- stans et vi- ctor su- is ap-

-rens di- le- cto- ri- bus vi- vus,

-pa- rens ____ di- le- cto- ri- bus vi- vus,

-pa- rens di- le- cto- ri- bus vi- vus, ____

-pa- rens ____ di- le- cto- ri- bus vi- vus,

17. Pri- mo Ma- ri- ae, de- hinc A- po- sto- lis, do- cens scri- ptu- ras, cor a- pe- ri- ens

ut clau- sa de i- pso re- se- ra- rent.

18. Fa- vent i- gi- tur re- sur- gen-

18. Fa- vent ____ i- gi- tur re- sur- gen-

18. Fa- vent i- gi- tur re- sur- gen-

18. Fa- vent i- gi- tur re- sur- gen- ti ____

19. Lu- cent cla- ri- us sol et lu- na, mor- te Christi tur- bi- da. Tel- lus her- bi- da

re- sur- gen- ti plau- dit Chri- sto, quae tre- mu- la e- jus mor- te se ca- su- ram mi- ni- tat.

20. Er- go di- e i- sta ex-sul- te- mus, qua no- bis vi- am

20. Er- go di- e i- sta ex- sul- te- mus, qua no- bis vi-

20. Er- go di- e i- sta ex- sul- te- mus, qua no- bis vi-

20. Er- go di- e i- sta___ ex-sul- te- mus, qua___ no- bis vi-

___vi- tae re- sur- gens___pa- te- fe- cit___Je- sus.

-am vi- tae___ re- -sur- gens pa- te- fe- cit Je- sus.

-am vi- tae re- sur- gens pa- te- fe- cit Je- sus. 21. A- stra, so- lum, ma- re

-am__ vi- tae re- sur- gens pa- te- fe- cit Je- sus.

ju- cun- den- tur, et cun- cti gra- tu- len- tur in cae- lis spi- ri- ta- les cho- ri to- nan- ti.

Communion *Pascha nostrum*

32

Mass for Whit Monday

Introit *Cibavit*

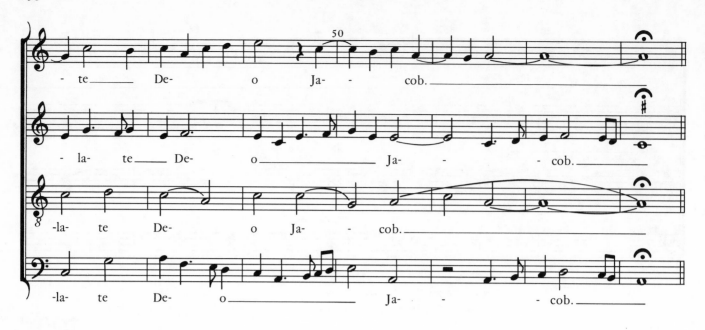

-te___ De- o Ja- cob.___
-la- te___ De- o___ Ja- - cob.___
-la- te De- o Ja- cob.___
-la- te De- o___ Ja - - cob.___

Glo- ri- a Pa- tri, et Fi- li- o et Spi- ri- tu- i San- cto, *Sic- ut e- rat in prin- ci- pi- o,

[D. C. al Fine]

et nunc, et sem- per, et in sae- cu- la sae- cu- lo- rum. A- men.

Alleluia *Veni Sancte Spiritus*

Al- le - - lu- ia. - lu- ia.___
Al- le - - lu- ia. - lu- ia.___
Al- le - - lu- ia. - lu- ia.___
Al- le - - lu- ia. - lu- ia.___

-ris in____ e- is i-
ris in e- is
-ris in____ e- is
-ris in____ e- is____

-gnem ac- cen- - -de. i- gnem ac- cen- - -de. i- gnem ac- cen- -de. i- gnem ac- cen- de.

42

Sequence *Veni Sancte Spiritus*

1. Ve- ni San-cte Spi- ri- tus, Et e-mit- te cae- li- tus Lu- cis tu- ae ra- di- um.

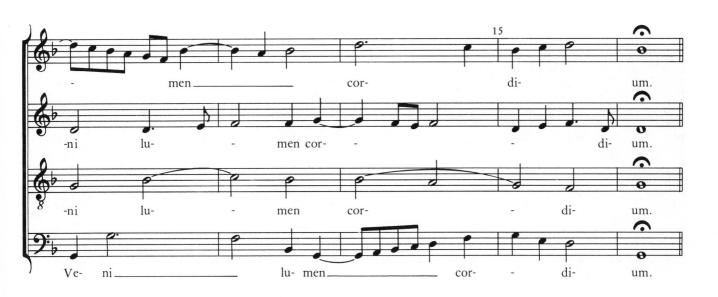

44

46

7. La- va quod est sor-di- dum, Ri-ga quod est a- ri- dum, Sa-na quod est sau-ci- um.

8. Fle- cte quod est ri- gi- dum, Fo- ve

8. Fle- cte quod est ri- gi- dum, Fo- ve

8. Fle- cte quod est ri- gi- dum, Fo- ve

8. Fle- cte quod est ri- gi- dum, Fo- ve

quod est fri- gi- dum, Re- ge quod est

quod est fri- gi- dum, Re- ge quod

quod est fri- gi- dum, Re- ge quod est

quod est fri- gi- dum, Re- ge quod

de- vi- um.

est de- vi- um.

de- vi- um. 9. Da tu- is fi-de-li-bus, In te con- fi-den-ti-bus,

est de- vi- um.

10. Da vir- tu- tis____ me- ri-

10. Da vir- tu- tis me- ri-

Sa-crum se-pte-na- ri- um.

10. Da vir- tu- tis me- ri-

10. Da vir- tu- tis me- ri-

-tum, Da____ sa- lu- tis____ e- xi- tum, Da pe- ren-

-tum, Da sa- lu- tis e- xi- tum, Da pe- ren-

-tum, Da sa- lu- tis e- xi- tum, Da pe- ren-

-tum, Da____ sa- lu- tis____ e- xi- tum, Da____ pe- ren ne____

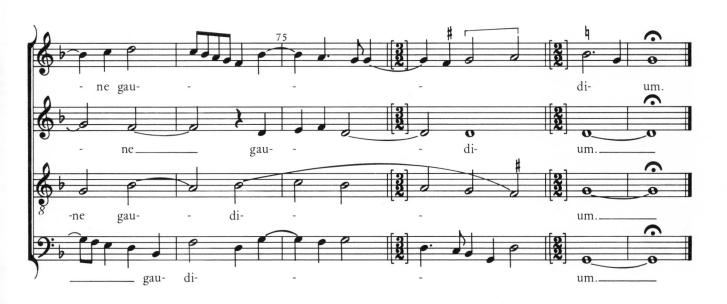

- ne gau- di- um.

- ne____ gau- di- um.____

-ne gau- di- um.____

____ gau- di- um.

48

Communion *Spiritus Sanctus*

Mass for Feasts of the Blessed Virgin Mary

Introit *Salve sancta Parens*

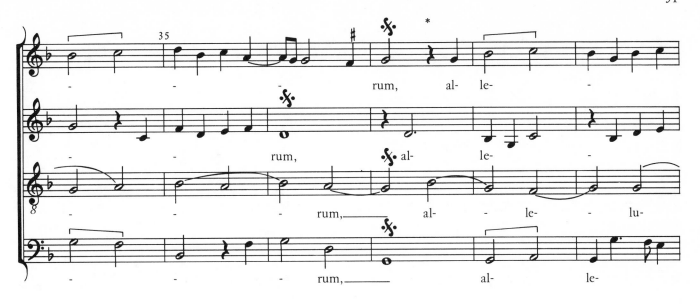

-rum, al- le-
-rum, al- le-
-rum, al- le- lu-
-rum, al- le-

[Fine]

-lu- ia.
-lu- ia.
-ia.
Verse
Sen- ti- at o- mnes tu- um le- va- men:
-lu- ia.

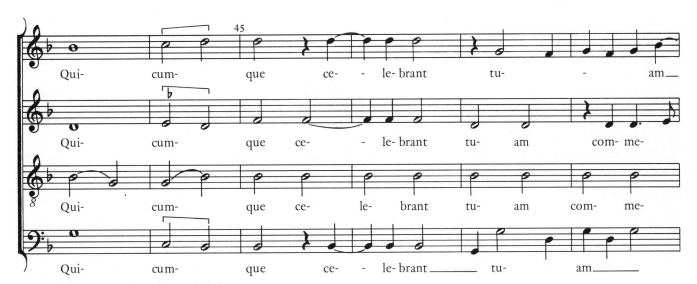

Qui- cum- que ce- le- brant tu- am
Qui- cum- que ce- le- brant tu- am com- me-
Qui- cum- que ce- le- brant tu- am com- me-
Qui- cum- que ce- le- brant tu- am

*The *alleluia* is omitted outside Paschal Time.

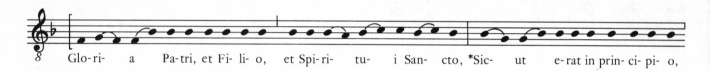

Glo- ri- a Pa- tri, et Fi- li- o, et Spi- ri- tu- i San- cto, *Sic- ut e- rat in prin- ci- pi- o,

[D.C. al Fine]

et nunc, et sem- per, et in sae- cu- la sae- cu- lo- rum. A- men.

Kyrie

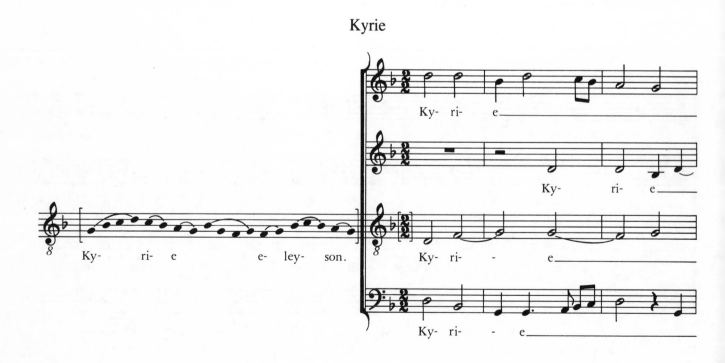

Ky- ri- e

Ky- ri- e

Ky- ri- e e- ley- son.

Ky- ri- e

Ky- ri- e

e- ley-

e- ley-

e- - ley- - son.

e- ley-

- son.

-son.

-son.

Ky- ri- e

e- ley- son.

Gloria *Spiritus et alme*

Glo- ri- a in ex- cel- sis De- o. Et in ter- ra pax ho- mi- ni- bus

58

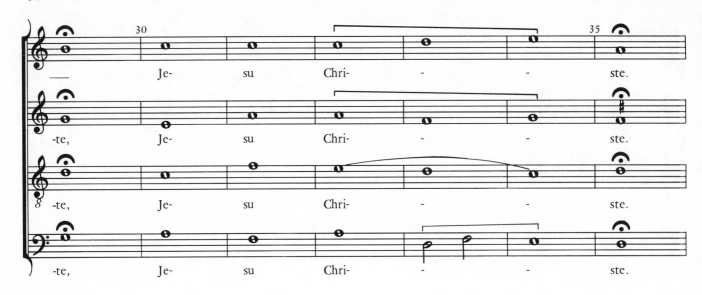

Je- su Chri - - ste.
-te, Je- su Chri - - ste.
-te, Je- su Chri - - ste.
-te, Je- su Chri - - ste.

Spi- ri - tus et al - me___ or- pha-
Spi- ri - tus_____ et al- me or- pha-
Spi- ri - tus et al- me or- pha-
Spi- ri - tus et al - me or - pha- no-

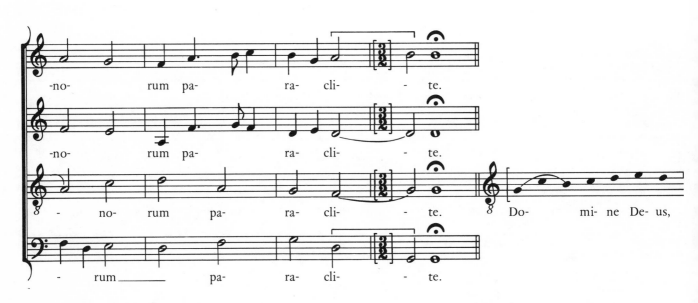

-no- rum pa- ra- cli- te.
-no- rum pa- ra- cli- te.
- no- rum pa- ra- cli- te. Do- mi- ne De- us,
- rum_____ pa- ra- cli- te.

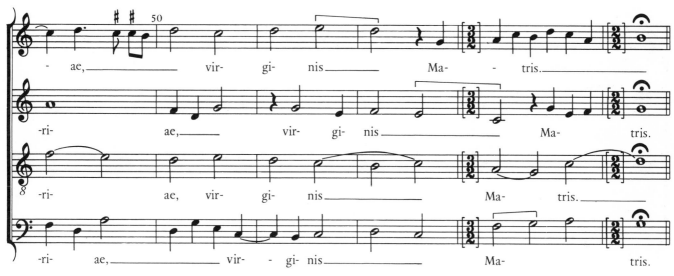

60

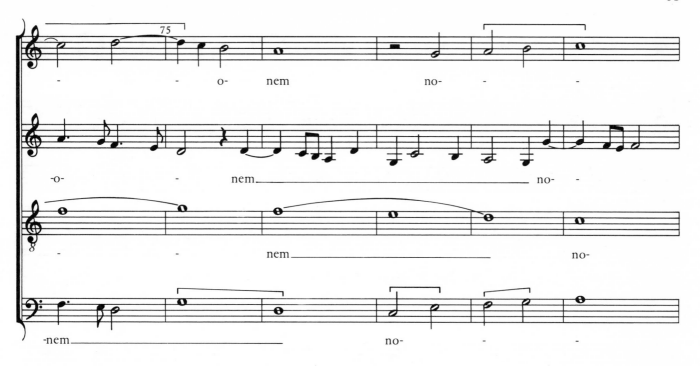

-o- -nem no- - -
-o- - nem no-
- - nem no-
-nem no- - -

-stram. Ad Ma- ri- ae glo- - ri- am.
-stram. Ad Ma- ri- ae glo- ri- am.
-stram. Ad Ma- ri- ae glo- - ri- am.
-stram. Ad Ma- ri- ae glo- - ri- am.

Qui se- des ad dex- te- ram Pa- tris, mi- se- re- re no- bis.

62

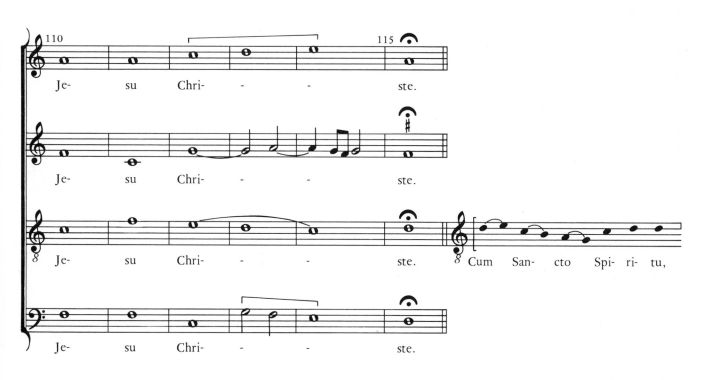

Alleluia *Virga Jesse*

66

68

Sequence *Ave praeclara maris stella*

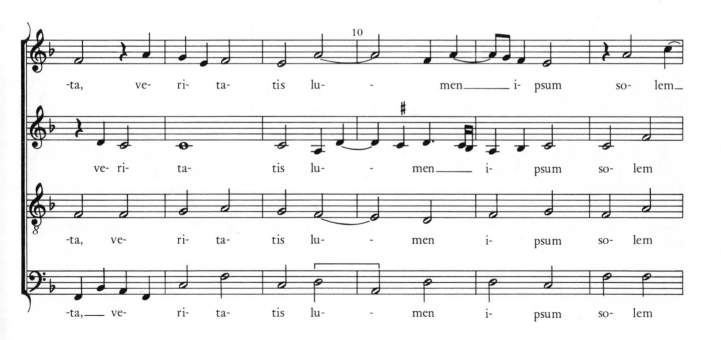

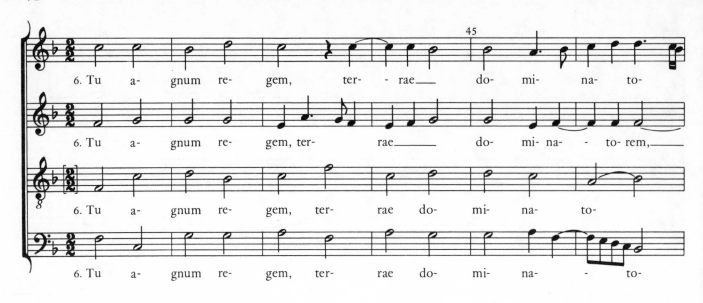

6. Tu a- gnum re- gem, ter- - rae___ do- mi- na- to-

6. Tu a- gnum re- gem, ter- rae___ do- mi- na- to- rem,___

6. Tu a- gnum re- gem, ter- rae do- mi- na- to-

6. Tu a- gnum re- gem, ter- rae do- mi- na- - to-

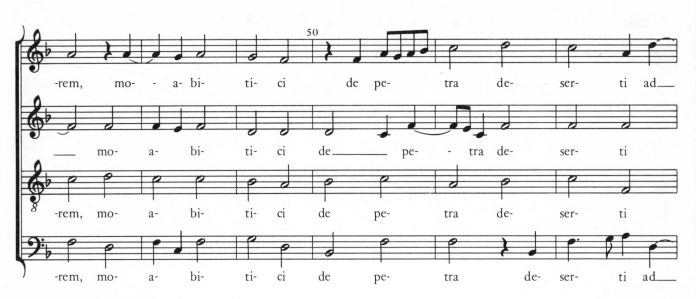

-rem, mo- a- bi- ti- ci de pe- tra de- ser- ti ad___

___ mo- a- bi- ti- ci de___ pe- tra de- ser- ti

-rem, mo- a- bi- ti- ci de pe- tra de- ser- ti

-rem, mo- a- bi- ti- ci de pe- tra de- ser- ti ad___

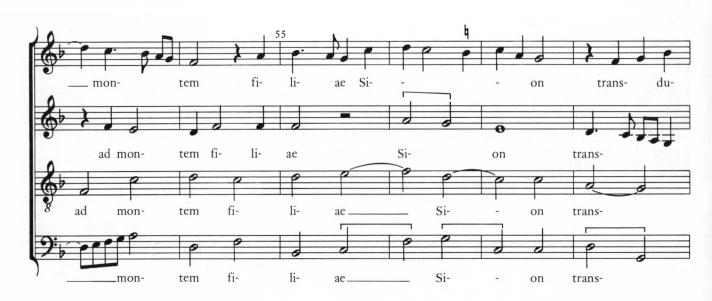

___ mon- tem fi- li- ae Si- - on trans- du-

ad mon- tem fi- li- ae Si- on trans-

ad mon- tem fi- li- ae___ Si- on trans-

___mon- tem fi- li- ae___ Si- on trans-

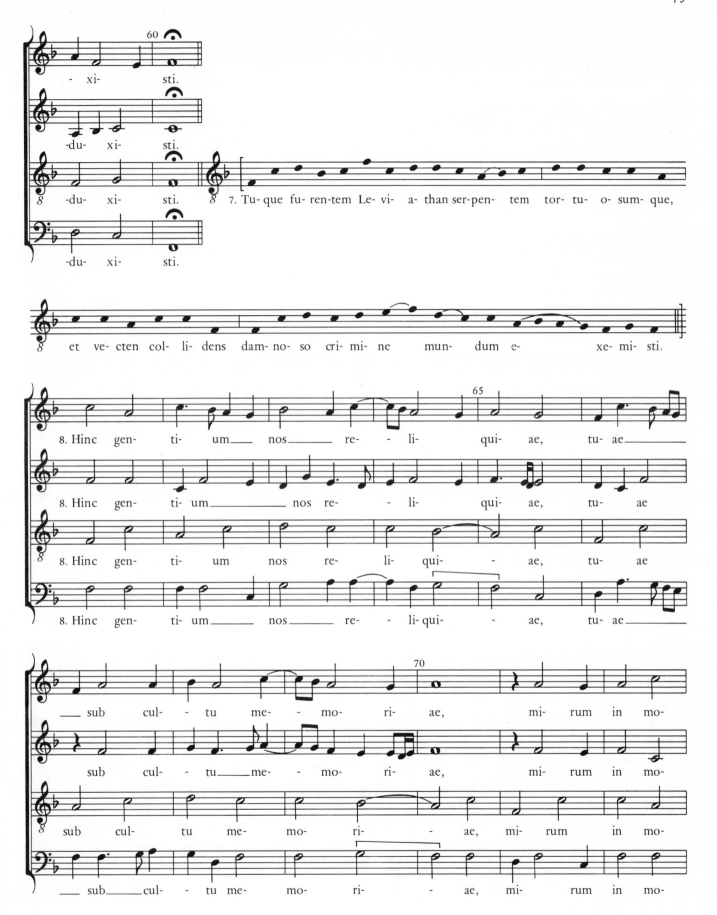

-xi- sti.

-du- xi- sti.

-du- xi- sti.

7. Tu-que fu- ren-tem Le- vi- a- than ser-pen- tem tor-tu- o- sum-que,

-du- xi- sti.

et ve-cten col- li-dens dam-no- so cri- mi- ne mun-dum e- xe- mi- sti.

8. Hinc gen- ti- um nos re- li- qui- ae, tu- ae

8. Hinc gen- ti- um nos re- li- qui- ae, tu- ae

8. Hinc gen- ti- um nos re- li- qui- ae, tu- ae

8. Hinc gen- ti- um nos re- li- qui- ae, tu- ae

___ sub cul- tu me- -mo- ri- ae, mi- rum in mo-

sub cul- tu me- -mo- ri- ae, mi- rum in mo-

sub cul- tu me- mo- ri- ae, mi- rum in mo-

___ sub ___ cul- tu me- mo- ri- ae, mi- rum in mo-

9. Hinc man- na ve- rum Is- ra- e- li- tis ve- ris, ve- ri A- bra- hae fi- li- is,

ad- mi- ran- ti- bus quon- dam, Mo- y- si quem ty- pus fi- gu- ra- bat, jam nunc ab- du- cto

ve- lo da- tur pro- spi- ci; o- ra Vir-go, nos il- lo pa- ne coe- li di- gnos ef- fi- ci.

10. Fac fon- tem dul- -cem, quem in_ de- ser- to pe- tra prae-mon-

10. Fac fon- tem dul- cem,_quem_ in_ de- ser- to pe- tra prae-mon-

10. Fac fon- tem dul- cem, quem in de- ser- to pe- tra prae-mon-

10. Fac fon- tem dul- -cem, quem in_ de- ser- to pe- tra prae-mon-

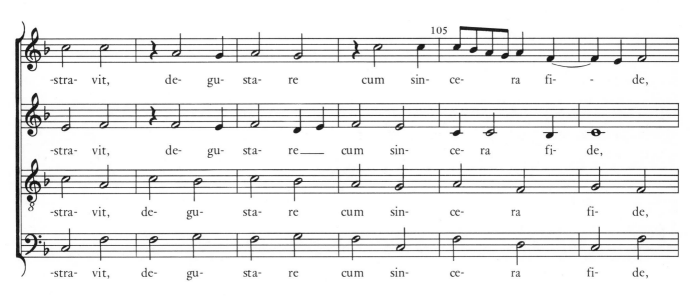

-stra- vit, de- gu- sta- re cum sin- ce- ra fi- - de,

-stra- vit, de- gu- sta- re_ cum sin- ce- ra fi- de,

-stra- vit, de- gu- sta- re cum sin- ce- ra fi- de,

-stra- vit, de- gu- sta- re cum sin- ce- ra fi- de,

re- nes- que____ con - strin - gi, lo - tos in ma- ri an-

re- nes- que con - strin- gi, lo- tos in ma- ri

re- nes- que con- strin- gi, lo- tos in ma- ri

re- nes- que con- strin- gi, lo- tos in____ ma- ri

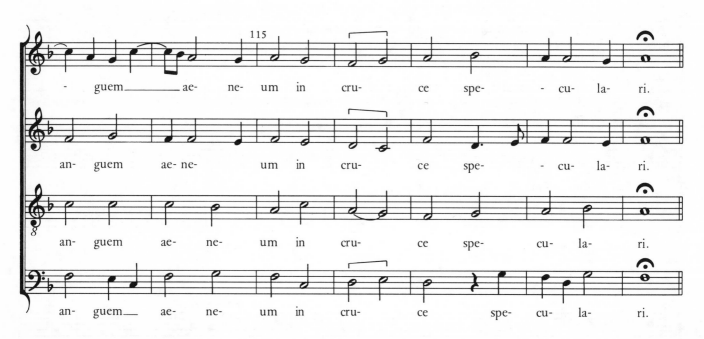

- guem____ ae- ne- um in cru - ce spe - cu- la- ri.

an- guem ae- ne- um in cru- ce spe - cu- la- ri.

an- guem ae- ne- um in cru- ce spe- cu- la- ri.

an- guem____ ae- ne- um in cru- ce spe- cu- la- ri.

11. Fac i- gni san- cto, pa- tris- que ver- bo, quod ru- bus ut flam- ma tu por- ta- sti,

Vir- go, Ma- ter fa- cta, pe- cu- a- li pel- le, di- stin- ctos pe- de,

-ros men- tis o- cu- los in te de- fi- ge- re.

-ros men- tis o- cu- los in te de- fi- ge- re.

-ros men- tis o- cu- los in te de- fi- ge- re.

-ros men- tis o- cu- los in te de- fi- ge- re.

15. Quo hau- sto sa- pi- en- ti- ae sa- po- rem vi- tae va- le- at mens in- tel- li- ge- re;

16. Chri- sti- a- nis- mi fi- dem o- pe- ri- bus

16. Chri- sti- a- nis- mi fi- dem o- pe- ri- bus

16. Chri- sti- a- nis- mi fi- dem o- pe- ri- bus

16. Chri- sti- a- nis- mi fi- dem o- pe- ri- bus

re- di- me- re, be- a- to- que fi- ne ex hu- jus in-

re- di- me- re, be- a- to- que fi- ne ex hu- jus in-

re- di- me- re, be- a- to- que fi- ne ex hu- jus in-

re- di- me- re, be- a- to- que fi- ne ex hu- jus

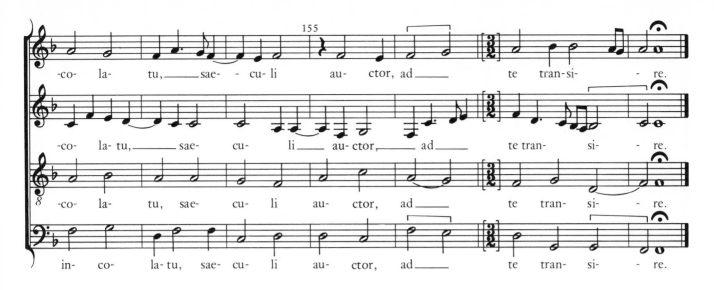

Communion *Beata viscera*